PONIES AND DONKEYS

PETS OF TODAY SERIES

PONIES AND DONKEYS

David Le Roi, MA, BSC, FIAL

Illustrated by
Persephone Jackson

KAYE & WARD
LONDON

First published in Great Britain by

Kaye & Ward Ltd
21 New Street EC2M 4NT, 1976

Copyright © Kaye & Ward Ltd 1976

Cased ISBN 0 7182 0402 6
Limp ISBN 0 7182 0404 2

Photoset by TRI-AM Photoset Ltd,
Bridge Foot, Warrington

Printed in Great Britain by
A. Wheaton and Co., Exeter

Contents

CONTENTS

LIST OF ILLUSTRATIONS

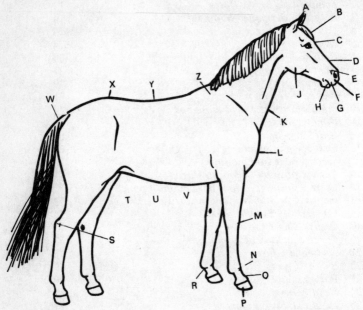

1. Anatomy of the pony: (A) ears; (B) forelock; (C) forehead; (D) face;
(E) muzzle; (F) nostrils; (G) upper lip; (H) lower lip; (J) cheek
bone; (K) throat; (L) breast; (M) knee; (N) fetlock; (O) pastern;
(P) hoof; (R) heel; (S) hock; (T) flank; (U) abdomen; (V) barrel;
(W) dock (root of tail); (X) loins; (Y) back; (Z) withers.

Chapter One

THE PONY'S ANCESTRY

There are few animal-lovers who would not like to have a pony as a pet. Unfortunately a pony can hardly be classed as a household pet and cannot be kept like a dog or a cat. There is, for example, the problem of housing and exercising, not to mention the cost of feeding. A pony cannot live in the house with you, and its exercise entails a great deal more than a short walk in the morning and evening; also it has a large appetite that cannot be satisfied with tinned foods and kitchen scraps.

Unless you live in the country with a nearby field for the animal to graze in, keeping a pony must be out of the question. A pony is certainly not the kind of pet to keep in a town or a city. There are, of course, town and city dwellers who own a pony, which they board out at a riding school or at a stable in the country, but that makes the pony a very expensive pet. Not only is there the cost of the animal's food and stabling but also visiting the pony when you wish to ride him means a journey that can be expensive in time and money. The next best thing to owning a pony is to hire one from a riding school, which may be found in or near most large towns. Although you could own your pony and board him at a riding school, it would cost a great deal more than hiring a mount.

Nevertheless, if you decide on the second best thing and are satisfied with just riding a pony without owning it, you will get a great deal more pleasure from your riding if you know something about ponies and how they should be treated. That is the purpose of this book.

But first, what is a pony? A pony is simply a small horse. This does not mean it is a small horse because it is a young horse but a horse that is small when it is fully grown. Horses are measured for size in a unit called a 'hand'. A hand is taken as being equal to 4 inches, and a horse's height is stated as being so many hands from the ground to the withers or top of the shoulder (see figure 1). Accordingly a pony is an adult horse which does not exceed 14 hands in height, i.e. it is not more than 56 inches from the ground to the withers. Some ponies can be as small as 8 hands or 32 inches.

Ponies and their bigger relatives, horses, have an ancestry dating back for millions of years. In fact, as we shall see, the biggest horses we know today are actually descended from animals smaller than the tiniest of modern ponies.

Very little was known about the ancestry of horses or ponies until 1836. In that year, William Colchester, owner of the Kingston brickworks in Suffolk, who was also an enthusiastic amateur geologist, dug out of a local clay deposit a fossil tooth. Colchester showed his find to a scientific friend who promptly dismissed it as being of no importance. Then in 1840, William Richardson, a professional geologist, was searching for fossils on Studd Hill, Kent, when he unearthed a small skull. Although uncertain of the species of animal to which the skull might have belonged, Richardson was inclined to identify it as that of a hare.

Throughout the next decade, several more unidentifiable fossils were discovered in Europe and in America. All these discoveries, including the Kingston tooth and the Studd Hill skull, had one thing in common: none of them bore any resemblance to the fossils of animals then known to scientists. After careful and prolonged examination of scores of the mystery fossils unearthed in Europe, America and Asia, scientists came to the conclusion that the fossils could only be the relics of an entirely new species of prehistoric animal.

The nearest animal anatomy in any way similar to that indicated by the fossils is that of the horse. Certainly the fossil
tooth and skull were those of some very small animal, probably
not much bigger than a hare, but the skull in particular was
surprisingly horse-like.

Eventually the scientists agreed that the fossils undoubtedly
were those of a small, horse-like creature. Judging from the
geological features of the ground in which the fossils had been
found, it was established that the mysterious little animal
probably roamed the earth about 65 million years ago. This
distant period of the world's past is called Eocene or, as it is
sometimes known, the Age of Mammals. From the many fossils
now available, zoologists have been able to reconstruct the size
and general appearance of the mystery animal. It was estimated
to have been a small, fox-like creature little more than 12 inches
high and with four toes on each fore foot and three toes on each
hind foot.

This first definite ancestor of the horse and the pony was
christened Eohippus or Dawn horse. According to the fossils,
Eohippus appeared almost simultaneously in Europe and in
what is now the American continent. Millions of years ago,
Europe and America were joined by a land bridge across what is
now the Bering Strait. For some reason the Dawn horses seem to
have migrated in large numbers from Europe to North America,
and it is in the latter continent that the horse passed through the
greater part of its evolution.

Throughout tens of millions of years, the horse gradually
changed in appearance and habits as it adapted itself to changing world conditions of geography and climate. It was ultimately
transformed into the animal we know today. Eohippus, for
example, had teeth adapted for eating only soft food. This
suggests that it lived in the forests which then covered so much of
the world's land surface, feeding on soft leaves and shrubs.

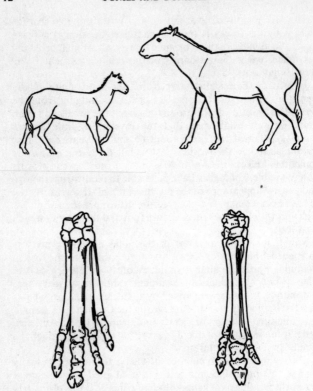

2. (Left) *Eohippus or Dawn Horse;* (below) *forefoot with its four toes;*
(right) *Merrychippus with* (below) *the forefoot with elongated
middle toe.*

Having neither claws nor horns to protect itself, Eohippus had to depend upon speed to escape the bigger predatory animals which hunted it. It had a good turn of speed, and the toes on its feet gave it a firm grip on the ground as it turned and twisted to escape its enemies.

With the passage of time, counted in millions of years, descendants of Eohippus were compelled to move into the grass plains or prairies as the world's forests became fewer and smaller. Throughout the whole history of evolution, nature has always been at pains to adapt small and defenceless creatures so that they can develop means of protecting themselves against bigger and more powerful enemies. That is what happened to the horse. Some ten million years after Eohippus appeared on earth, the little fox-like ancestor of the horse had developed into a bigger animal called by zoologists Merrychippus whose middle toe on each foot was much larger, while the other toes were considerably smaller. Whereas Eohippus had small cusped teeth ideal for chewing soft leaves, Merrychippus had grinding teeth with ridges designed for cropping tough grass.

Some three million years ago, Merrychippus evolved into another species of horse-like animal called Pleohippus. This animal was bigger and could run much faster than Merrychippus. The side toes of the feet had become much smaller and a definite hoof was evolving.

After Pleohippus there were many more evolutionary changes in the horse's ancestry, and all the changes followed a regular pattern. The animal was definitely evolving into a horse. It was becoming bigger and much faster than its tiny forebears, while its relatively high eye-level enabled it to have a better chance of spotting the many voracious enemies that hunted it on the open plains. Apart from increasing size, the most remarkable development in the horse's evolution throughout tens of millions of years was the structure of the feet. The centre toe,

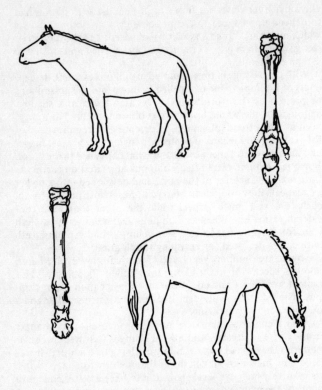

3. (above) *Pleohippus;* (right) *centre toe of foot is developing into single hoof;* (below) *later development of Pleohippus; the foot (left) has almost completed development into a hoof, while the side toes are little more than vestigial relics.*

which bore most of the animal's weight when running, grew bigger and bigger, while the outside toes became smaller and smaller. What was eventually left was the single enlarged toe which we call a hoof. Raising the animal's body on a central toe or hoof gave the developing horse an exceptionally good turn of speed and ensured the specie's survival in face of the horde of predators that beset it. With the development of the hoof, there

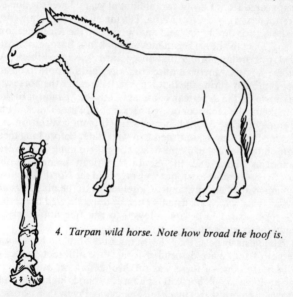

4. *Tarpan wild horse. Note how broad the hoof is.*

occurred further modifications of the teeth to make them suitable for cropping and chewing the coarse grasses and shrubs on which the animal depended for its food.

Pleohippus was the true and direct ancestor of the modern horse. From Pleohippus have evolved every one of the great varieties of horses now existing throughout the world. Pleohippus is the ancestor of the Clydesdale and Shire, just as much as he is the ancestor of the tiny Shetland pony.

The ancestors of today's horses and ponies have had a somewhat chequered history. Fossil remains suggest that they disappeared from Europe for millions of years. Later the horse's forerunners vanished from Asia. During all this time, however, the horse was developing and multiplying on the American continent. Then the horse began moving back into Europe and Asia by way of the land bridge that once joined Alaska to Siberia. As for the horse's American ancestors, they all disappeared from that continent during the first Ice Age. Thereafter the horse was unknown on the American continent until the Spaniards took it with them when they conquered Mexico and Peru. Descendants of some of these Spanish horses strayed from civilization and became ferel: that is, returned to a wild state. Before long there were huge herds of semi-wild horses roaming the North American plains and the South American pampas. Comparatively few now exist, but they provided the North American Indians with their mustangs. Closely akin to the mustangs are the broncos, which are usually born by domesticated horses but are then turned loose and allowed to run free until they are wanted for breaking-in.

Zoologists believe that the riding and draught horses and ponies of today are descended from three different species of wild horse. One of these was the Mongolian or, as it often is called, Przewalski's horse. It is about 13½ hands high and is light brown in colour with a black tail and mane. Przewalski's horse is now almost extinct in its wild state, though there are a few very small herds still roaming the Mongolian steppes.

Many of the horses used for riding, particularly in North

Africa and in the Mediterranean countries, trace their descent from the tarpan. The tarpan was a small, light-boned animal about 48 inches (12 hands) high at the shoulder. It was distinguished by a very broad forehead and an exceptionally stiff mane. Tarpans once roamed in vast herds across the plains of Europe and Eurasia. Though the tarpan is now generally said to be extinct, there are reports of a few wild specimens occasionally being sighted in the more desolate regions of Eurasia.

Heavy draught horses have an obscure ancestry. Some experts believe them to be descended from a cross between the tarpan and Przewalski's horse.

In these days of fast road, rail and air travel, we are apt to forget just what an important part the horse and the pony have had in thousands of years of man's history. But the surprising thing is that man's first interest in the horse was not as an animal to ride or to carry or haul his goods. Prehistoric man's only interest in the horse was as a source of food. Horses that ran free when man was evolving from an ape-like creature into a human being were more than a match for our prehistoric ancestors. Man's crude weapons were generally ineffectual when used for hunting the speedy, agile and ruggedly-strong wild horse. Then, as weapons improved, man was occasionally able to bring down a wild horse and feast on its flesh. Stone Age cave paintings never depict the horse as a mount or as a beast of burden, but always as a game animal like the reindeer, bison and wild boar. The bones of horses found outside the ancient cave-dwellings in Solutré near Lyons in France prove that the men of the Old Stone Age ate horse flesh. The bones had all been split for the extraction of the marrow.

History does not record when or where the horse and pony were first used as riding or draught animals. The earliest indication of the horse as a domestic animal consists of a bridle and a few parts of a metal harness found in a Bronze Age deposit established as dating from approximately 2500 BC. One of the earliest pictures of what appears to be a domesticated horse forms part of a cave drawing in southern Sweden which was executed some 4,000 years ago.

The earliest written references to domesticated horses consist of a few brief inscriptions on Babylonian clay tablets which were inscribed in about 2300 BC. According to the inscriptions, the use of the horse as a beast of burden was restricted to a few nomadic tribes. By 1700 BC the domestic horse had become common throughout the Euphrates and fast horses were used in the Babylonian army to draw the archers' chariots. In this connection it is interesting to note that for centuries after the horse had been domesticated there are no records of it ever being used for riding. Its sole role was that of a pack animal or as a drawer of vehicles. Even the Ancient Egyptians, who fully appreciated the speed and strength of the horse and developed the horse-drawn chariot into the most devastating weapon of the ancient world, seldom rode the animal. There are only a few vague references to cavalry in the writings of the period. To the Egyptians the horse was merely the motive power for a chariot. Certainly they never employed horses for hauling loads or dragging ploughs – there were always hordes of human slaves for such tasks.

Wherever the horse has been pressed into man's service it has made a tremendous impact on his way of life. Once man had learned how to break in the horse and pony, great quantities of goods could be carried over long distances either in waggons or on horses' backs. From the primitive waggons hauled by the first horses to wear harness developed the well-sprung coaches and carriages which in time led to the building of good roads for them to run on. For thousands of years the horse-drawn coach was the fastest vehicle on land until the invention of the steam locomotive little more than 150 years ago. Until the building of the railways, the horse was the backbone of all postal systems and was the means of carrying despatches and mail. Nearly 3000 years ago, the Greek historian Herodotus wrote admiringly of the Persian organization of fast horses ridden by the couriers who delivered government letters and dispatches.

It was, however, the military use of the horse as a riding animal that had the greatest influence on man's history. War chariots and cavalry soldiers changed the whole concept of military tactics and strategy. It was the cavalry horse that enabled Alexander the Great to achieve his far-flung conquests. Without horses to ride, the ravaging hordes of Attila and Alaric could hardly have ventured out of Asia let alone have pressed on into Europe to humble the Roman Empire. Though the armies of Genghis Khan consisted of the best organized and best trained troops the world had seen since the fall of Rome, the Tartar conqueror reached the gates of Vienna only because he was the leader of half a million invincible mounted soldiers.

The Crusaders were no less dependent upon their horses. Indeed, until the advent of infantry armed with firearms, the cavalryman was virtual master of the battlefield. In the days of chivalry it was the heavy breed of horse from northern Europe that carried the massively-armoured knight into battle. That the cavalryman on his horse remained invincible when pitted against an enemy without firearms was proved as late as the sixteenth century when Spain conquered South America. When Cortez landed in Mexico, he had only sixteen horses. Yet with that small force of cavalry he conquered the Aztec Empire. Admittedly terror among the enemy had much to do with the Spaniards' easy victory: the Aztecs had never seen horses before, and imagined that a horse and rider were one creature with superhuman powers.

Until the invention of the steam locomotive and the internal-combustion engine, the horse was the quickest form of transport on the road. But the coming of the motor vehicle ended the horse's long reign of supremacy. Had it not been for the ever-increasing popularity of riding for pleasure, it is doubtful whether either horses or ponies would now be seen anywhere except on a race course.

Chapter Two

MEET THE PONY FAMILY

There are over 60 different breeds of pony throughout the world. With some there is very little distinction between one breed and another. On the other hand, there are some obvious dissimilarities: you would not, for instance, fail to tell the difference between a Shetland pony and a New Forest pony. The following list is a form of pony *Who's Who*: it will give you some idea of what a particular breed of pony looks like and where it comes from. Many of the ponies listed you may never see, but you will be regarded as a knowledgeable person if you are able to talk about Galicenos, Kirghiz, Senners and other lesser-known breeds. The height given for the various breeds is that of the average stallion.

AMERICAN PONY. Bred from the Arab and typical cowboy's round-up horse. It often has speckled flanks and rumps. 11 hands.

AVELIGNESE. First bred in Italy, the Avelignese is a big, strong and extremely healthy pony, but it is very docile and easy to train. 14 hands.

BALI. Native to Indonesia, this strong sturdy pony is suitable for both pack and riding. Generally of a dun colour with a black dorsal stripe, mane and tail. 13 hands.

BASUTO. Native to Basutoland, Africa, and descended from Arab and Barb horses. Usually chestnut, bay and brown with,

21

occasionally, white markings. It may be distinguished by its comparatively short legs and exceptionally hard hooves. 14 hands.

BATAK. A native of Indonesia, the Batak is a hard-working pony and very docile. It has Arab blood and appears in most of the usual colours. 12 hands.

CAMARGUE. Native to the Camargue region of the Rhone delta, this pony is found semi-wild in the bleak, watery region around Arles. Accustomed to rough pasturage, it is strong and easy to feed. It is used as a cow-pony for guarding the herds of Camargue cattle. Usual colour grey. First bred by the Romans from Arab and Berber horses. It makes a good riding pony but is inclined to be temperamental.

CHINA PONY. Bred in China from the Turkestan and Mongolian pony, it is small and hardy with a thick neck, deep chest and very hard hooves. The mane is very coarse, while the tail is often long enough to sweep the ground. Exceptionally strong and healthy, it is used for riding and load-carrying. One of the fastest of ponies and claimed to be faster than an Arab, it is trained for racing. Dun is the most common colour with black-tipped ears and black tail. 12 hands.

CHINCOTEAGUE. First bred in the Chincoteague Islands off the Virginia coast, U.S.A., by seventeenth-century English settlers, the animal is more horse-like, particularly in the head, than the average pony. Strong and hard-working, the Chincoteague is often piebald or skewbald.

CONNEMARA. First bred in Connaught. A first-class riding pony with exceptionally strong limbs, it is even tempered and very easy to train. Colour dun with black tail, mane and dorsal stripe. It has some Spanish blood in its ancestry. 13 hands.

CRIOLLO. This variety was first bred in Peru from the Spanish horses brought to that country by the conquistadors. Besides being a first-class riding pony with an exceptionally graceful gait, it is used on ranches as a cowboy mount. Usually dun, sorrel, grey or black in colour. 13 hands.

DALE. One of the oldest breeds in Britain having been used as pack animals in Celtic times. It is still used for sheep-herding on farms in the Dales. Colours brown or jet black with white markings. An excellent riding pony. 14 hands.

DARTMOOR. An old-established breed native to Dartmoor in Devon. Breeds in semi-wild herds on crags and moorlands. It is a hardy, reliable and fast pony, ideally suited to riding. 12 hands.

DULMAN. One of the two breeds of pony native to Germany. It runs in a semi-wild state, the youngsters being annually rounded up and sold. They are first-class riding ponies and very hardy. 12 hands.

EXMOOR. Oldest of England's native ponies, it was used by the Celts for their chariots and as a pack animal. It is an exceptionally intelligent pony to ride and is one of the best pony jumpers. It is characterised by its heavily-hooded eyes and runs semi-wild in Exmoor, Somerset. 12 hands.

FELL. A very old breed of native English pony. Besides being an all-purpose working pony on the Fell farms, it is popular as a riding pony. 13 hands.

FJORD. One of the few breeds of pony which today have any resemblance to the horses of the Ice Age. A good riding and working pony, it is very stout-hearted and was bred by the Norsemen for pony fighting. It is cream or yellow on its body with a dark mane and stockings.

5. Exmoor pony.

FULANI. Bred by the Fulani tribesmen of Nigeria and the Cameroons. The Fulani are nomads and use the ponies for riding and as pack animals. 14 hands.

GALICENO. A Mexican pony used for harness, riding and ranch work. It is probably descended from the horses brought to Mexico by the Spanish invaders. A slim but strong pony with a good turn of speed, it is usually black, bay or dun. 12 hands.

GOTLAND. Sometimes called the Skogsruss, the Gotland was first bred in Gotland, Sweden, from a Syrian mare and an Arab stallion. Although inclined to be obstinate, the pony is in great demand for farm work. It is also a good riding pony and in some parts is specially bred for trotting races. The coat comes in most horse colours, and the mane and tail are inclined to be straggly. 12 hands.

6. *Highland pony.*

HACKNEY. One of the most perfect of all the pony breeds, it is ideal for driving or riding. It has an exceptionally graceful action and is specially bred in Great Britain for shows. 12 hands.

HAFLINGER. Originally bred in Bavaria and now popular in Austria, it is the ideal pony for mountain work with either pack or saddle. It is often used to pull sleighs in Germany and Austria. The coat is nearly always chestnut with a flaxen mane and tail. 14 hands.

HIGHLAND. Largest and strongest of the British ponies, they are native to the Scottish mainland and the western isles. They make good riding ponies and are noted for their docility. Being extremely strong, they are much used by the highland crofters for riding and as beasts of burden. Exceptionally sure-footed, they are unrivalled for hill work and in mountains. 13 hands.

HUZUL. A Polish bred pony. Willing, strong and tireless, it is an excellent mountain pony for pack or saddle. 12 hands.

ICELAND. Introduced into Iceland from Norway in the ninth century, this pony lives in semi-wild herds. A tough and gallant animal, the Iceland is a strong and dependable mount of amazing staying power. Its sturdy legs are rarely subject to the ailments common to horses and other ponies. It is remarkable for its mane which is often double-sided and for the thick hair on the tail. It grows a thick grey, dun, black or chestnut coat in winter. 12 hands.

KATHIAWARI. Native to the Kathiawar and Murwar provinces of India, it is exceptionally strong and tough, and is popular as a saddle or pack animal in hilly country. The Kathiawari is one of the oldest breeds of pony and prehistoric remains found in the Silwalik district suggest that there were ponies of the Kathiawari type in India long before they found their way to Europe.

KIRGHIZ. Bred in the Kirghiz region of the Soviet Union, it has remarkable stamina as a pack or riding pony, and, because of its sure-footedness, it is popular in mountain districts. 14 hands.

KONIK. A good riding and draught pony, the Konik is claimed to be the nearest domesticated relative of the Tarpan wild pony. It was the foundation of nearly all Russian and Polish ponies. The coat is yellow, grey or blue dun. Koniks are particularly even tempered, willing and long-lived. 13 hands.

KURDISTAN. As its name implies, a breed native to Kurdistan, Turkey. Although excellent for riding, most of the Kurdistans in Turkey are used in agriculture as pack and draught animals, and for trampling or threshing corn. They are noted for their slim and graceful but very strong legs. 12 hands.

MANIPUR. Named after the state in India where it has been bred for thousands of years, this breed is fast and easily trained. Manipurs are frequently used as polo ponies. 13 hands.

7. *New Forest pony.*

NEW FOREST. New Forest ponies are mentioned in the *Doomsday Book* of 1086 and for centuries have run semi-wild in the New Forest. Properly broken-in and trained, it is an excellent riding pony for children. The coat is any colour except piebald or skewbald. 12 hands.

NEW ZEALAND. General name given to any type of pony bred in New Zealand. Most of them are descended from stock imported from Australia.

NIGERIAN. Hardy and willing pony bred in Nigeria. Used for riding and draught, it shows a distinct Barb strain. 14 hands.

NORLAND. This hardy pony is almost unknown outside Norway, where it is bred for riding and draught. It is probably descended from the Mongolian and Tartar ponies. It has a dark coat with a long tail and mane. 13 hands.

PECHORA. This strong, hard-working and docile pony is virtually unknown outside its native Russia. Its amazing endurance enables it to travel up to 40 miles a day on the most simple of diets. 13 hands.

PENEIA. Breed of pony local to Peneia in the Peloponnese. Strong and easy to feed, it is a first-class riding and draught animal. 14 hands.

POLO. The polo pony has been bred from a number of breeds to produce a muscular, fast and obedient animal, instantly responsive to its rider's wishes. A polo pony makes an excellent saddle animal for the ordinary but experienced rider. 14 hands.

PRZEVALSKI. This is the wild pony of the Mongolian steppes

which survives in much the same form today as it did in the Ice Age. The ponies have been greatly reduced by hunting and encroachment on their haunts so that less than 50 specimens are now left in the wild state. In fact there are more of them in zoos. Distinguished by a stripe down the back, an upright mane and zebra-like markings on the upper parts of the forelegs. It is not used for riding. 13 hands.

QUANTOCK. Bred from Exmoor-pony stock, it was introduced into the Quantock hills in the west of England about a century ago.

8. *Shetland pony.*

SABLE ISLAND. A draught and saddle pony popular in Canada. They come from Sable Island off the coast of Nova

Scotia. They are extremely hardy and on Sable Island, where they live semi-wild, they successfully survive extreme winter conditions, digging scrub grass from under the snow and breaking the ice on fresh-water ponds for drinking. 14 hands.

SANDALWOOD. The native pony of Indonesia. They are beautifully proportioned ponies with a soft shining coat. They are splendid for riding and in Indonesia are used for bareback racing.

SENNER. Although the Senner is an exceptionally hardy pony and an excellent mount, it is practically unknown outside the Teutoburg district of Hanover, Germany. 12 hands.

SHAN. Bred along the mountain borders of Kashmir and Nepal, the Shan is remarkable for its short, quick steps. Despite its often sleepy look, it is a very alert pony and appears to enjoy walking along the narrow paths on mountainsides. 13 hands.

SHETLAND. Although the strongest of the pony tribes, the Shetland is the smallest, sometimes less than 9 hands. At one time it was widely used for drawing trucks in coal mines. It is now the most popular pony for children. It is an ideal pet and, when properly treated, develops a dog-like affection for its master or mistress. The coat, which can be of any colour except skewbald or piebald, is very thick in winter, but fine and sleek in summer.

SKYROS. Breed native to the Aegean island of Skyros. It is used locally as a water-carrier and for threshing corn, but it is popular throughout Greece with pony clubs teaching children to ride. 10 hands.

SORRAIA. The native pony of Portugal, this tough pony can successfully survive in extremes of weather and on the poorest of pastures. It is used mostly as a pack animal in Spain and Portugal. Its coat is dun with a dark dorsal stripe and stripes on its legs. 14 hands.

9. Welsh Mountain pony.

SUMBA. This highly intelligent and willing pony is bred in Indonesia and is best known for its dancing performances. Ridden by small boys and with bells attached to their forelegs, they dance to the rhythm of drums. The Sumba pony is usually dun colour with a dark stripe along the back, and a black or deep-brown tail and mane. 12 hands.

TIBETAN. Native to Tibet, this strong and active pony is suited by its strength and hardiness for pack and saddle work in the rugged country of the Himalayas. 12 hands.

TIMOR. This delightful little pony deserves to be better known outside its native Indonesia. Despite their small size, they are excellent mounts for rounding up cattle. The Timor's hardiness and docility would make it an excellent pony for children.

VIATKA. Native to the Baltic districts, this strong and docile pony is equally happy with a rider or pack on its back, or drawing a cart or sleigh. 13 hands.

WELSH. Claimed to be the supreme pony of the show ring, the Welsh has an exceptionally even temperament, making it an ideal mount for children. 12 hands.

WELSH COB. Another old English breed. It is descended from the Welsh Mountain pony and was crossed with Spanish warhorses to become the mounts for King Richard I's knights. It is a good harness and saddle animal.

WELSH MOUNTAIN. The Welsh Mountain pony has the longest recorded history of any breed native to Britain. Julius Caesar founded the first stud at Laka Bala, Merioneth. The ponies are bred in the Welsh hills and mountains in a semi-wild state, though many now come from private studs. Welsh Mountain ponies have outstanding endurance and are exceptionally intelligent.

Chapter Three

POINTS ABOUT BUYING A PONY OR DONKEY

This chapter is primarily for those who are in the fortunate position of being able to buy a pony and, if they live in the country, keep it at home. Alternatively, you may live in a town and buy a pony to be kept at a riding school or livery stable within fairly easy reach of your home. Incidentally, the advice offered in this chapter applies equally to donkeys and ponies. But first a piece of serious and well-meant advice. If you do not live in the country but you want to own a pony, do consider very carefully where you are going to keep the animal. How far from your home will the stable be? It may mean that you can see or ride the pony perhaps for only one day a week. Keeping a pony at a suburban livery stable or riding school and seeing it once a week is not going to help you get to know the animal very well.

The greatest joy of owning a pony or a donkey, or any other animal for that matter, lies in establishing a close relationship with the animal, and in gaining an understanding of its ways and its likes and dislikes. Only then can you develop the close relationship that makes for a happy animal and a happy owner. Remember, too, that the kindest of 'landlords' boarding a pony may well have other animals in his charge. With the best intentions in the world he will not have the time to devote to your pony in order to give it the personal affection and attention which mean so much to an animal. Moreover, neither a pony nor a donkey is going to feel any particular affection for someone it sees only once or twice a week, and then just to be taken out for a short ride. Only through regular watering, feeding, grooming and exercising by you will the animal accept

33

you as an essential part of its life. It is not going to be very interested in you as an occasional visitor.

You will have to bear in mind, too, the economics of ownership. In these days of inflation and unstable prices it is not possible to give exact figures for the cost of a pony or donkey and the expense of its feeding and accommodation. A reasonably good pony that has been broken in may cost well in excess of £100, while its board and lodging will be not less than £5 a week. In this connection it is important to remember that the nearer the pony's quarters are to a town, the higher will be the cost of boarding and feeding it.

If all these problems facing the town-dweller proposing to own a pony cannot be solved, I would advise you most strongly to be content with hiring a pony from a riding school or livery stable. Both you and the pony you ride will be more content.

Before buying a pony you should be able to ride. Obviously you will want to try a potential purchase to get the general feel of the animal and to find out how it responds to reins and knees. If you try to do this without being able to ride, your introduction to a pony is liable to end in disaster. Later in this book I will be giving you some brief hints on riding.

As already pointed out, investing in a pony is not cheap. Therefore knowing something about what a healthy pony should look like and how it is likely to behave when ridden will save you a lot of money, time and disappointment. Learning to ride at a riding school can be a great help when you come to acquire a pony of your own. Most riding instructors are only too happy if a pupil is enthusastic enough to want to own a pony. That being so, have a talk with your instructor. He will be able to give you much helpful advice and, as he taught you to ride, he will be able to recommend the kind of pony which he thinks will suit you best.

Some riding schools have ponies for sale and, if you can buy one this way, many of your problems may be solved. The school may not have a pony suitable for you at the moment, but your instructor will most probably promise to watch out for an animal that will meet your needs. He will also bear in mind the price you or your parents are prepared to pay. There is, however, one important point to think of when considering the purchase of a pony that has been used for riding lessons: the animal may not be very young and, as it has probably been used for scores of different pupils, it may find difficulty in adjusting itself to one particular person. On the other hand, it may be a young animal that is being sold because it shows the beginning of some bad habit. Fortunately, very few riding schools would risk their reputation by trying to sell to a pupil or former pupil a pony that is past its prime or is thought to be developing vices, so do not hesitate to seek the advice of your instructor when you contemplate owning a pony.

If the riding school is unable to get you a suitable pony, you will have to start looking for one yourself. There are several ways of doing this. You may have a friend who has a pony for sale or your friend may know where to find one. This is often the most satisfactory method of purchase, since a friend is hardly likely to be associated with the sale of a vicious or unhealthy pony. The pony or the seller may be known to the local pony club. If you cannot find the address of the local club, write to the British Horse Society at the National Equestrian Centre, Stoneleigh, Kenilworth, Warwickshire. Pony clubs are offshoots of the British Horse Society, and the latter is always willing to give new owners and riders encouragement and advice. Another likely source of information for prospective owners is the Ponies of Britain Club, Brookside Farm, Ascot, Berkshire.

When writing to a club or to a society, please remember to enclose with your letter a stamped envelope addressed to yourself. Clubs and societies depend for their income on subscriptions from members and, in these days of high postal rates, having to pay the postage on every reply to a query can be a serious expense.

Other likely sources of ponies for sale are newspapers, especially local ones, and the magazines devoted to horses and riding. Although advertising managers of reputable newspapers and magazines do their best to ensure that the statements and claims made in For Sale columns are accurate and truthful, never buy a pony or a donkey on the strength of what an advertisement says. Advertising managers are not generally pony experts, and they can take action only when they discover that a published advertisement contains misleading information. You are usually on safer ground when an advertisement appears in a riding or pony magazine. You will find the following magazines most helpful:

Pony, 19 Charing Cross Road, London WC2. *Pony* is published monthly. It is fully illustrated and caters specially for young riders. Besides advertising ponies for sale, it carries articles and notes about the feeding, care and riding of ponies, together with other valuable hints and instructions. There are also articles about ponies throughout the world and informative replies to readers' letters.

Riding, 189 High Holborn, London WC1. This is another useful magazine which is published monthly. It covers all aspects of riding and publishes very informative instructional articles on pony management and breeding.

Horse and Hound, I.P.C. Magazines, 189 High Holborn, London WC1. This weekly magazine does not specialize on the pony as much as *Pony* and *Riding*, but its advertisements include ponies for sale.

Many a good pony has been bought from a horse-dealer. Once upon a time the horse-dealer had a dubious reputation, but the dishonest dealer is in the minority today. Before buying through a dealer, try to find out something about him. This is where your riding instructor and the local pony club will be of help. In any event, an established dealer has a reputation to consider. As much of his business depends upon the recommendations of customers, it is unlikely that he would deliberately sell you a bad pony or donkey.

Unless you have some knowledge of ponies, it is unwise to buy one at the so-called horse fairs held in country districts. Gypsies who attend these fairs are acknowledged pony experts, but many of the dealers with ponies for sale are rogues without a drop of gypsy blood in their veins. A lot of the so-called gypsies at fairs are no more than shady salesmen of the 'here today and gone tomorrow' type. Unless a dealer calling himself a gypsy can be vouched for by someone you know and trust, avoid him like the plague. All he is interested in is collecting your money and then disappearing before you find out just what a wretched animal has been foisted on you.

Any reputable dealer who does not have the type of pony you want will invariably be willing to find a suitable animal. Tell him how much riding experience you have had and the limit you are prepared to pay. It is best to quote a figure rather less than that which you are willing to pay. This gives you some room to manoeuvre if there is any bargaining to be done.

When the dealer produces a pony you fancy, ask him if he is willing to let you have it on trial for a week. Reputable dealers are usually agreeable to this and will take back a pony which you find to be unsuitable. Having a pony on trial has obvious advantages. Let the animal have a couple of days to get accustomed to his new surroundings, then try riding it.

Finally, before deciding on a purchase, ask your local veterinary surgeon to give the pony or donkey a thorough examination to test its wind, limbs and eyes, and to estimate its age. The pony probably is offered to you with what is called a vet's certificate of the animal's age and soundness. Nevertheless, it is always wise to have a second veterinary opinion.

Ponies are generally sold under what is known as 'warranty'. This is a statement from the seller, either written or verbal, that the animal he is selling to you is sound in health and is suitable for the purpose for which you want it. Wherever possible, insist on a written warranty since this carries much more weight if the pony falls short of the warranty and becomes the subject of legal action. Read very carefully any written warranty offered to you with a pony or, for that matter, with a donkey. Make certain that the document covers everything: the age of the animal, its soundness in wind, limb and sight, and, above all, its freedom from vices. This latter is particularly important if the pony or donkey is to be ridden by a child. The following is a typical warranty given in the form of a receipt:

Received from (name of purchaser) the sum of £.... for a (colour of animal) pony stallion (or mare) of .... hands warranted .... years old, sound, free from vice and quiet to ride.

Signed (seller's signature)
Date

You will notice that here the warranty consists of a description of the pony following the word 'warranted'. Had the warranty read '. . . 12 hands, 10 years old and sound, warranted free from vice and quiet to ride', the age and soundness of the pony would not have been warranted.

Although it would be foolish and completely irresponsible to buy a pony from anyone without first having the animal examined by your veterinary surgeon, you will find that buying a pony is much more interesting if you have some idea of what to look for in a healthy and well-disposed animal. In the very nature of things, vets are disinclined to give a clean bill of health to an old pony. Yet it is quite possible that a pony between 8 and 10 years is the ideal mount for a beginner. An older pony is less likely than a young one to have vices such as kicking, biting, or rearing or shying for no reason at all. Above all, an older pony is much less liable to be nervous or excited when ridden in traffic. So have a talk with your vet. If he tells you that the only thing that prevents him from giving a pony or donkey a clean bill of health is its age, there is no reason why you should not buy it. Of course, if the vet informs you that a prospective purchase is suffering some defect due to old age, reject the animal at once.

There are a number of reliable indications of an animal's age and state of health. You cannot judge a pony's age by its appearance. Many an old pony that has been well cared for all its life looks considerably younger than its actual years. Conversely, a young pony that has been neglected frequently looks older than it really is. While on the subject of pony age, remember that all ponies and horses have an official birthday, irrespective of the actual date on which they were born. Thus the age of thoroughbreds is dated from the 1st January of the year in which they were born. Other ponies have their age dated from the 1st May in the year they were born. From this you will realize that the natural age of a pony can be up to 11 months before or after its official birthday. Terms used to denote a pony's age are:

COLT   A young uncastrated pony, that is a young male pony that has not been neutered.

FILLY   A young female pony.

FOAL   A pony under 1 year old.

YEARLING   A pony 1 year old.

STALLION   A male pony over 3 years old.

MARE   A female pony over 3 years old.

PONY   General name for a pony of either sex, but, in its precise meaning, a stallion.

Two other important pony descriptions are GELDING and ENTIRE. A gelding is a male pony that has been castrated or neutered, i.e. a gelding cannot breed. Entire means an ungelded pony stallion.

Sometimes you will see a pony's age described as 'rising 4'. This means that the animal is nearer 3 years old than it is to 4. 'Off 4' means that the pony is nearer to being 4 years old than it is to 3. When a pony is described as 'aged', it means that it is over 8 years old. Do not be discouraged from buying a pony which you otherwise find suitable merely because it is described as aged. Many a pony of 8 years can have 10 more years of useful life in front of it.

One of the most reliable indications of age is teeth. The normal adult male pony has 40 or 42 teeth, while an adult female has 36 or 38 teeth. The variation in the number of teeth between the sexes is explained by the fact that the small 'wolf' teeth are sometimes absent. The lower number of teeth in the mare is because she does not have canine teeth. Unfortunately, only an expert can tell you a pony's age from its teeth. The various factors indicating age by teeth are far too complicated for the amateur. Consequently, unless you are an expert, it is very easy to err on one side or the other of the animal's real age, so I do not propose to deal in this book with tooth standards.

It is sometimes claimed that a pony's age can be established by hollows above the eyes and that these deepen as the pony grows older. This indication is most unreliable since the depth of the hollows can vary from one pony to another irrespective of age.

Before you decide to buy a particular pony, watch the animal carefully while it is on the move. If the pony takes short little steps, something may be wrong with the animal's feet. The trouble is probably *laminitis* or foot fever, which is caused by excessive growth of the horn on the outside of the hoof, giving the whole hoof a kind of dish-shape. Provided the condition is not too pronounced, it can be remedied by keeping the excess horn well pared back and by protecting the sole of the foot with a piece of leather and fitting the hoof with a carefully-made shoe. Nevertheless, unless you are prepared to spend considerable time and money on veterinary fees, I would recommend rejecting a pony that is obviously suffering from laminitis of the hoof. Laminitis causes a pony's feet to become painful when it trots, hence the characteristic short, little steps. The pain is relatively slight on soft ground, but it is intense on hard ground. Not only is this cruel to the pony but it is also extremely uncomfortable for anyone riding the animal.

Another and much more serious foot ailment is *navicular*. It is so-called because it affects the navicular bone in the foot. The complaint is usually betrayed by the pony resting the affected leg in a forward position. Confirmation of navicular can be obtained by examination of the pony's shoes. If part of a shoe shows excessive signs of wear in relation to the rest of the shoe, it may well be caused by navicular. Although there are various methods for the relief of this disease, it tends to get worse. As there is little hope of a cure, reject any pony showing symptoms of the complaint.

A fairly common defect in ponies is called *splints*. This is a condition of the main bone of the leg. It can be detected by a small lump felt when you run your fingers down the leg bone. Normally splints is not a very serious matter, but, if the lump is large, it can be the cause of future lameness, particularly if the lump is midway down the inside of the leg. Your veterinary surgeon will confirm whether the pony has splints or not and if it is serious enough to justify rejecting the animal.

The tendon running down the back of a pony's leg is easily sprained. A *sprain* often can be detected by running your fingers and thumb down the back of the leg bone. If you can feel your fingers against your thumb, the tendon is free of any sprain. But any suggestion of puffiness indicates some inflammation, which may be due to a sprain. Reject a pony showing pronounced puffiness, as the animal may be liable to sprains. Sprains are difficult to treat and can lead to permanent lameness.

Soundness of wind is essential in a healthy pony or donkey. Put simply, unsound wind is merely another term for shortness of breath when a pony exerts itself, as when galloping or cantering. It manifests itself as a whistling noise when the animal comes to rest. The louder the whistling, the more unsound it is in wind. Another indication of unsound wind is a double heaving of the flanks while the pony is breathing. A broken-winded animal may have serious respiratory trouble. It is sometimes caused by allowing the animal to get too fat, and may be halted by reducing the quantity of the animal's feeds. There is a temporary form of unsound wind caused by working the animal after it has had a heavy meal.

Your veterinary surgeon will have little trouble in telling you if a pony is permanently broken-winded, or if the condition is temporary and can be cured by attention to diet and work. But it is as well to remember that a permanent unsoundness of wind is often progressive and generally incurable, particularly if it indicates some respiratory complaint. If the veterinary surgeon is at all doubtful, be on the safe side and reject any pony showing the slightest symptoms of unsound wind.

Having chosen your pony or donkey, you now have to pay for the animal. The normal arrangement is to pay the seller a proportion of the cost as a deposit. The balance of the payment is then made on, or just before, delivery of your purchase. Additional charges such as veterinary fees and transport of the pony from the seller to your stable or other accommodation are your responsibility.

If you can possibly manage to do so, complete the transaction in two payments: deposit and final payment. You can, of course, spread payment over a number of instalments through a finance house, but in this case there will be interest charges to be added to the original purchase price; and do not forget that, until the final instalment is made, the animal remains the property of the finance house. In the event of instalments not being paid, the pony or donkey can be repossessed by the finance house.

You may be able to buy the pony or donkey with a loan from your bank, but you will have to offer some security other than the animal. There will be, too, interest charges on the bank loan.

Chapter Four

STABLING

I will now assume that you are fortunate enough to have bought a pony or donkey and propose to stable it at or near your home. This being so, you will have to look after your animal to ensure that its life with you will be happy, comfortable and healthy. Never forget that owning a pony or a donkey means that you are accepting a responsibility. You must be prepared to devote considerable time to grooming and feeding, and to attending to all the other chores such as stable cleaning which ownership entails. Keeping a pony or donkey is not just a matter of having an animal to ride; it means daily tasks to look after an animal that is entirely dependent upon you for its well-being.

All too often a pony given to a child becomes a nine-days' wonder. After the first enthusiasm, the novelty wears off and the life of the pony or donkey becomes one of neglect and unhappiness. Eventually father or mother takes pity on the animal and is compelled to accept responsibility for it. This is not the way to be a successful owner of any animal. Unless a child fully understands that the animal is his and is, therefore, his responsibility, it is best not to allow a youngster to have a pony or a donkey. He or she must be content with riding ponies hired from a livery stable or a riding school.

As I have said, this chapter is primarily for the guidance of those who are going to own a pony or a donkey and stable it where they will be able to look after it themselves. Nevertheless the chapter will, I hope, be useful to those who do not yet own a pony or a donkey, but who may one day be fortunate enough to do so.

44

If you are going to accommodate your pony or donkey in conditions essential to its health and comfort, a proper stable is vital. Do not imagine for one moment that a disused garage or an old garden shed will do; the animal must have proper stabling. Ideally, the stable should be of brick with a tiled roof, but with the ever rising cost of bricks and tiles, not to mention labour, the cost will have to be counted in hundreds of pounds. Alternatively, a suitable existing building can be converted or you can buy a sectional building to be erected on the site. Whichever of these is decided upon, however, it is not going to be cheap and will definitely cost considerably more than the pony or donkey.

Before building or otherwise setting up a stable, you must submit to the local council or other authority detailed plans of the proposed building, together with exact and full particulars of the location and site. The plans must indicate the precise position of the proposed stable, not only in relation to your own property but also in relation to your neighbours' property. Most local authorities have strict regulations about stabling and these must be rigidly adhered to.

It would be a wise precaution to find out as much as possible about any proposed new roads in the district. You do not want to go to the expense of building a stable only to discover that the powers-that-be are thinking of making a compulsory purchase order so that the stabling can be demolished as the site is on the line of a new motorway.

Should you be foolish enough to set up a stable without consulting the appropriate authorities, a court order can be obtained compelling you to pull down the building at your own cost. Fortunately few authorities want to be deliberately obstructive. If you approach them properly and show that you are willing to accept their reasonable requirements and decisions, you will find them co-operative. They will tell you what is at fault with your plans and will indicate which site for the proposed building will be the most acceptable.

A stable can be of wood, brick or stone. Although brick and stone stables are the most costly of all, they could be cheaper in the long term and will last for many years with the minimum of maintenance. Brick and stone do, however, tend to be cold in winter. Breeze blocks are almost as durable as brick and stone, but the walls must be rendered inside and out with a good covering of cement to make them damp-proof.

I have seen so-called stables built from sheets of corrugated iron over a timber framing. I would never recommend this form of structure, as it makes a very cold stable for winter. Another disadvantage of corrugated iron is that the noise made by rain or hail battering against it is liable to frighten the animal.

Stables built of plain planking or feather boarding nailed to a timber frame are not really satisfactory since they cannot be proof against wind and rain. Draughts, incidentally, are the cause of many equine upsets. The only use for feather boarding in a stable is for interior lining; this will keep the animal warm and will protect it from draughts.

There is only one efficient use of timber for the main walls of a stable, and that is in the form of heavy boarding which is deeply tongued and grooved to exclude draughts. This type of boarding also makes an excellent lining for a brick, stone or breeze-block stable. All timber used for stabling should be thoroughly creosoted on the exterior to render it weather- and rot-proof, while interior woodwork should be coated with a non-poisonous paint. White is a good colour, as it makes the inside of the stable bright and cheerful.

Careful thought must be given to the choice of roofing material for a stable. Thatch is probably the best, as it keeps the interior of the building warm in winter and cool in summer. Unfortunately thatching is rapidly becoming a dying craft and it is, in consequence, far too expensive. Another disadvantage is that thatching will harbour unwanted insects and it is liable to be a fire risk. This latter can be an important consideration when it comes to insuring the building.

Corrugated iron is, in my view, the worst possible choice for a stable roof. Apart from the noise created by hail and rain beating on it, a metal roof induces damp through condensation, and damp conditions are very bad for the health of a pony or donkey.

One of the best roofs is made from heavy tongued and grooved boarding, covered with thick, tarred felt. Alternatively, the boarding can be covered with one of the mastic compounds. This will make the roof absolutely waterproof.

Not the least important part of a stable is the floor. This can be of concrete or of cement-bonded brick. There is one drawback to a brick floor: if the cement bonding cracks or flakes, which it well may do under the pounding of the animal's hooves, water and urine will seep through, so that the floor is always damp. Personally, I would prefer a concrete floor, providing the materials are properly mixed and laid to a depth of about 9 inches. The concrete should be laid on a good foundation of rubble from which all the earth has been sifted. It will add to the strength of the floor if steel mesh is laid between the concrete and the foundation. A concrete floor should have a very slight slope from either side to a shallow central groove or gulley, while the whole floor should slope slightly from the stall area to the door. These slopes will ensure that water and urine drain away and do not collect all over the floor. The central gulley or groove in the floor must be shallow, about 10 inches wide and without sharp edges. Observing these precautions will prevent the animal from tripping or slipping on the gulley.

To prevent the ground in front of the stable from becoming sodden, liquid from the gulley should be led through pottery piping for disposal at some distance from the building. Wherever possible, waste liquids from the stable should go through piping to the main sewer, but any connection to a main sewer must have the approval of the appropriate governing authority.

10. *Prefabricated stable of the loose-box type. Note ventilation louvres and half doors. This stable will accommodate a pony and a donkey, or two ponies or two donkeys.*

There are available various types of prefabricated stable which are relatively cheap and quite efficient. They are, however, seldom as satisfactory as a stable erected on the site by a qualified builder. The chief point in favour of prefabricated stables is that they are easily and quickly erected by comparatively unskilled labour. The only really hard work associated with them is the laying of the floor. A cheap and efficient type of prefabricated stable is illustrated in figure 10; it is of the loose-box type and can accommodate two animals. This is an advantage in that stabling can be shared with someone else who owns a pony or donkey and lives near you. It also benefits the ponies or donkeys. Both are essentially herd animals and enjoy the company of their own kind. The prefabricated stable is a speciality of Gregory's Sectional Buildings Ltd, Uxbridge, Middlesex.

When two animals are housed in the same stable, it is essential that each has its own loose-box. The loose-box is, in effect, a separate room in which each pony or donkey can move about relatively freely. When animals are tied in stalls and their movement is restricted, they get very bored with nothing to see except a blank wall. On the other hand, in a loose-box the animal can look over the lower part of the door and see what is going on outside. Boredom generated by stall stabling is a common cause of a pony becoming vicious and developing various bad habits. Whenever possible, therefore, a pony should be housed in a loose-box stable. The loose-box must be roomy enough for the animal to turn round freely without bumping against walls. More important still, the loose-box must be big enough for the pony or donkey to lie down when it wants to and then get on its feet again. Actually more space is needed for the animal to get on to its feet than for it to lie down. If it finds difficulty in getting up, it will be discouraged from lying down at all and a pony or donkey must lie down occasionally if it is to get proper rest. Equally important, the loose-box must be high enough for the occupant to throw up its head without hitting the roof or rafters.

To meet all these requirements, a loose-box suitable for an average size pony should have a minimum area of approximately 8 square feet and a height of about 8 feet to allow for any tendency to rear on the hind legs. The door should be about 6 feet high and 4 feet wide.

Good ventilation is of paramount importance in a stable, but it must be ventilation without risk of draughts. Both these requirements are best met by means of louvres fitted just below the roof at each end of the building. Glazed windows are also essential, because the animals like to see around the interior of their quarters. Moreover, a stable into which little daylight enters has a very depressing effect on ponies and donkeys.

Ponies and donkeys need plenty of fresh air if they are to stay healthy, therefore the top section of the loose-box door should be kept open in fine weather. To maintain an adequate supply of fresh air in winter without draughts from open doors, the stable windows should be of the hopper type. This kind of window is hinged at the bottom and opens inwards against a shield on either side of the window frame. With this kind of window the incoming air is forced upwards without creating a draught. When the incoming air eventually descends, it diffuses with the air already in the stable and is warmed, so that the stable maintains a comfortable temperature. Foul air will then escape through the louvres.

Large quantities of ammonia vapour are produced in a stable from urine and other sources. Adequate ventilation is essential to carry away the vapour, which quickly fouls the air and, if allowed to concentrate, irritates the animal's mucous membranes and so induces colds.

Stable furniture and other fittings should be kept to a minimum. Avoid having wooden rack mangers fixed to a wall. Not only are they difficult to keep clean but also seeds and dust are liable to fall into the animal's eyes when it reaches up to feed. By far the most hygienic and safe food container is a small galvanized iron bath. It has no corners to harbour dirt. It should be removed and kept outside the stable after the pony or donkey has fed. Never feed hay by throwing it loose on the floor. If you do, it is soon trampled on and gets dirty and damp. The best way to feed hay is from a net tied in a corner of the loose-box.

Finally, a word about locking the stable door: the best way to secure the door of a loose-box stable is to have a ball and socket catch at the top of the half-door, and a bolt towards the bottom. The reason for having the bolt at the bottom is that, if it is at the top, a bored animal is quite likely to worry at it until it manages to slide the bolt out. The upper half of the door should close downwards and then be secured by a bolt on each side.

11. *Small boarded stable suitable for a donkey. There is a window in the wall facing the door.*

Chapter Five

THE EQUINE MENU

Ponies and donkeys are not particularly fussy about their food, neither do they require any specialized or particularly expensive items on their menu. The chief precaution is not to let the animal overfeed itself. An overfed animal not only becomes grotesquely fat, but it is more liable to develop ailments such as laminitis or foot fever. There is a very true saying among pony people that the ribs of a properly fed pony should be felt but not seen! And that can be achieved only by correct feeding. The staple, all-the-year-round feed for a pony or donkey is made up of hay, bran and oats.

Oats are by far the most nutritious of all grains fed to ponies and donkeys. The animals particularly relish oats, and they contain high protein and energy value, and are easily digested. They also have very valuable tonic properties. The most suitable oats are the white variety, which should be hard and dry with the minimum of husk. This latter is essential as the husks tend to be indigestible, as proved by the fact that they will appear in the animal's droppings. Oats are best fed in crushed form and can be purchased as such. If you cannot get crushed oats, the ordinary kind should be boiled or steamed until the husks split. Whenever possible, however, it is best to buy the ready-crushed grain since boiling the oats tends to destroy some of the valuable vitamins they contain. Boiled or steamed oats should be fed only when the crushed variety is unobtainable as too much boiled food can be the cause of stomach distention.

Hay is an exceptionally valuable food for ponies and donkeys, and in emergency it can be their sole diet. But it lacks sufficient energy-generating properties for animals eating nothing else to perform hard work. Clover and meadow hays are the most nutritional, and old hay is preferable to new. The disadvantage of new hay is that it is still in the process of making and undergoing chemical changes, which may lead to digestive troubles. Incidentally, old hay is hay which was gathered after 29 September (Michaelmas Day). Strictly speaking, hay is old 6 to 18 months after cutting. Hay older than 18 months must be avoided because it loses much of its nutritional value.

The distinction between new, old and too-old hay emphasises the importance of buying forage from a reputable chandler or dealer. It is wise to consult an experienced owner of a pony or donkey as to where he or she buys fodder and then order yours from the same source. Of course, if you live in the country, your hay problems are solved by getting in touch with a local farmer who raises livestock. He will generally have enough hay available for sale to supply the needs of your pony or donkey.

There are one or two simple tests whereby you can judge the quality of hay. Prime meadow hay is soft to the touch, and should not be a pronounced yellow in colour. Clover hay is more brittle to the touch. Whatever the kind of hay, avoid any that shows black or dark brown patches: this is an indication of dampness, which could cause stomach troubles. Hay with excessive dust should be avoided as should hay containing a lot of thistle, dock, sorrel and other weeds. Provided the dust is not excessive, the hay can be fed to the donkey or pony provided it is sprinkled with water before being given. *Under no circumstances sprinkle with water a complete store of hay containing dust*: this will only make the whole stock mouldy.

Some people chaff or cut up the hay they feed to their animals. This practice cannot be deprecated too strongly as an animal fed with chaff will not masticate properly and will tend to overeat. The only satisfactory method of feeding hay is uncut. Donkeys and ponies prefer it that way. To prevent uncut hay being fouled or wasted, never throw it on the floor for the animal to feed on at will. The uncut hay should be held in a net hung in the stall or loose-box. Hay can be bought in trusses of 60lbs or in bales of 80lbs.

There are a number of foods fed to ponies and donkeys which, though good for horses engaged in heavy work, are quite unsuitable for animals used for riding or kept as pets. Amongst these feeds you should avoid maize, beans and peas. Maize is too rich in carbohydrates and, unless the animals are doing a lot of strenuous work to use up energy, makes for excessive fat.

Blue, white and grey peas and soya and field beans can be given occasionally as a treat, but when fed regularly to ponies and donkeys they will lead to overheating. Being rich in protein, peas and beans make a useful addition to the diet of animals which may have to spend the night out of doors, particularly in winter.

Linseed, which is the seed of the flax plant, is another addition to the menu which should be given sparingly. In fact, linseed should be regarded as a tonic rather than as a feed. Given in moderate quantities, linseed is a good coat-conditioner and is invaluable for animals which have been ill and need fattening up. You will often find that a pony or donkey which goes off its normal feed will regain its appetite when given a small ration of boiled linseed.

Other items of diet which can be fed to ponies and donkeys, but only in small quantities additional to the normal menu, are barley, wheat and rye. These are best given after they have been ground and cooked.

There are a number of proprietory foods which combine in one feed all the protein and mineral content essential to a balanced diet. They also have the advantage of containing certain essential vitamins which are added during manufacture.

Called cubes or nuts, these proprietory foods are somewhat expensive, but their convenience may be considered to outweigh their cost. An animal does quite well on a menu of good hay and a ration of cubes or nuts. The containers in which they are sold usually give full directions as to how they should be fed to the animals.

Unless a pony or donkey is suffering from some form of tooth trouble which makes chewing difficult, mashes of the various grain foods should be fed very sparingly. The trouble with too much in the way of mashes is that the animal tends to swallow them without masticating. As a consequence the gastric juices do not function properly, so that digestion is incomplete and stomach upsets result.

A diet that consists solely of cereals and hay or of hay and cubes tends to become monotonous, and can result in a pony or donkey going off its feed. Some variation containing root vegetables will help to restore a jaded appetite. A daily ration of 3lbs of roots is always a welcome addition to the equine menu. Amongst suitable root vegetables are mangolds, carrots, turnips and swedes. The 3lb ration can be made up from a mixture of several different roots or it can consist of just one type of root. The roots should be sliced, grated or pulped before being given to the animal. *On no account should carrots be cut into discs*, since they have been known to cause choking when fed in that form. Unless the carrots are being mashed or grated, they are best cut into strips lengthwise. Although potatoes have little nutritional value in pony or donkey diets, they are usually greatly appreciated when given as raw slices. The ration should be limited to one large potato.

Ponies and donkeys which are seldom put out to graze need a daily ration of fresh grass, when this is possible. Never give an animal lawnmower cuttings as these can lead to colic. Any grass fed to a pony or donkey must be freshly cut. Grass starts heating and so begins to ferment soon after cutting; and fermented grass can lead to all manner of troubles when fed to an animal.

Salt is essential in a pony or donkey diet and it is common practice to leave a block of salt or a salt lick in the stall or loose-box. I would never recommend this, because constant licking at salt often results in the animal developing an uncontrollable habit of licking anything in reach, including the woodwork of its stall or loose-box. From constant licking it is but a stage to constant chewing, so that a pony or donkey may end up with splinters in its lips or gums. *The only safe and satisfactory way to give the animal salt is to sprinkle it on its food.*

I well remember a pony I had as a boy developing blood-poisoning after chewing at its loose-box and getting a splinter embedded between the gum and a tooth. Despite all the efforts of a veterinary surgeon, the pony had to be put down. The fatal chewing habit had developed from constant licking of a salt block in the loose-box. It provided me with a never-to-be-forgotten lesson on the dangers of salt blocks or licks.

The quantity of food required by a pony or a donkey depends to a great extent on the size of the animal, and how often and how long it is going to be ridden or otherwise worked. As it is impossible here to estimate with any accuracy the food requirements of a particular animal, you should ask the advice of the person from whom you acquired the pony or donkey. He will not object to giving you a diet sheet, and that, together with the recommendation of the veterinary surgeon who examined your purchase, should give you all the information you need about the size of feeds.

Irrespective of the amount of food recommended, remember that, if a pony or donkey is to get the best out of its food, the feeds given should be small and given at regular intervals. Giving a pony or donkey a complete day's ration all at once is asking for trouble. Divide the total amount of feed for a day into 4 and allow about 4 hours between each feed. The reason for spreading feeds is that a pony's stomach is small in relation to its size and cannot cope with large amounts of food at once. Nevertheless, ponies and donkeys are inclined to be very greedy and, given too much food at a time, they will take the opportunity to gorge themselves. An animal that gorges itself is certain to develop digestive trouble.

The first feed of the day should be given as early as possible, certainly not later than 8 am, while the last feed, mainly of hay, should be given between 10 and 11 pm. *Under no circumstances should a pony or donkey be ridden for at least one hour after a feed.* Failure to observe this rule means that the animal does not have time to digest its food properly, and that means trouble. If it is essential that an animal be taken out before an hour has elapsed after a feed, its pace must be restricted to a walk. Following a feed, the stomach becomes distended, and any exertion limits the free action of the animal's lungs so that its wind will suffer. Working a donkey or pony immediately after a feed runs the risk of its stomach being ruptured. *It is equally important not to give an animal its feed the moment it returns to the stable.* Neglecting this rule can induce stomach upsets as the animal is tired and its digestive system has not had enough time to begin functioning properly.

Ponies and donkeys, particularly the former, are thirsty creatures and must have an adequate supply of fresh drinking water, but that does not mean that water should be in the stable permanently, otherwise the animal will drink before feeding and that is extremely bad for it. An excess of water in the stomach before a feed means that the food will swell and possibly bring on an attack of colic. Moreover, excess water in the stomach while the animal is feeding means that a proportion of the cereal being given will be washed out of the stomach undigested. Any water in the stable should be removed one hour before feeding.

Then offer a short drink just before the feed to lubricate the works, so to speak.

Leave some water in the stable overnight. The animal's last feed will have been hay and this tends to raise a thirst. Do not leave too much water for 'nightcaps' – between 1 and 2 gallons will be enough for the average pony or donkey. If you can afford to, installing some form of controlled water-supply for night drinking will prove a good investment. One such system is the press-button drinker. This consists of a bowl which is filled from a storage tank when the button is pressed by the animal's nose. It is surprising how quickly a pony or donkey learns to press the button for a drink when it feels thirsty. Another system is a bowl kept filled with water from a tank fitted with a floating ball-valve, rather like that which flushes the domestic lavatory. The water supply to both systems can be cut off when the animal should not be drinking.

In spring and summer, when grass is at its lushest and most nutritious, ponies and donkeys should be put out to graze as often as possible. This is a fairly simple matter when the animal is kept out of town. Many farmers will be quite willing to let you graze your pony or donkey on one of their pastures. You will, of course, be expected to make some payment for the use of the pasture. There is no veterinary objection to grazing ponies and cattle together. One great advantage of being allowed to graze your animal on farm pasture is that you know that the farmer will not have sprayed the grass with fertilizers or herbicides harmful to animals. If permitted to do so, ponies and donkeys are liable to revert to the habits of their wild ancestors and to graze continuously. They must be prevented from doing this, otherwise, being gluttons, they will overfeed themselves and have digestive trouble. It is best to limit grazing to a few hours in the day. Also, ponies and donkeys allowed to graze must have their stable feeds reduced accordingly.

While on the subject of grazing, do not allow your animal to browse on roadside verges while you are out riding. Much roadside grass is seriously contaminated by deposits from diesel and petrol fumes released from the exhausts of motor vehicles.

Some ponies and donkeys kept as pets are allowed to live in a field all the year round. Although the summer grass provides them with enough nutritious food, it does not suffice in winter, when stable feeds have to be given. Also, some kind of shelter is necessary in bad weather. Shelter is necessary too in summer, otherwise the animal will be pestered by flies and other insects. On balance, it is best for the animal to be properly stabled throughout the year and allowed controlled grazing in summer.

Chapter Six

GROOMING AND STABLE CHORES

The appearance of domestic animals living in close association with man is a sure indication of their owner's attitude. This is particularly true of ponies and donkeys. An animal with a ragged coat, unkempt mane and tail, dirty hooves and worn shoes is proof that the owner does not care much for the animal as such, but simply as something to ride or otherwise put to work for its keep. *When you keep an animal you must accept full responsibility for its well-being.* An animal's well-being is not merely a matter of feeding and housing, it includes keeping the animal and its living-quarters clean. So, before you embark on buying a pony or donkey, do remember that the animal will have to be regularly groomed and its stable mucked out and cleaned. Stable cleaning can be hard and unpleasant work, but it has to be done.

To appreciate just how important grooming is to the general comfort of a pony, some knowledge of the structure and function of the skin and coat is necessary.

Ponies and donkeys have two skins. The first, or underlying skin, is called the dermis. It contains the blood vessels, nerves, sweat and oil glands, and the roots of the hair. The dermis is extremely sensitive to exterior sensations, injury and changes in temperature. Over the dermis is the upper or top skin, which is called the epidermis. The epidermis is dry and relatively insensitive, and is regularly shed in the form of scurf. Scurf is nothing more than finely-flaked epidermis skin.

The function of the sweat glands in the dermis is to maintain the animal's body temperature at a comfortable level. Sweating also helps to throw off some of the body's waste products. The purpose of the oil glands in the dermis is to waterproof the coat by slightly greasing it. In general, riding ponies work harder and move faster than do wild horses or those roaming in herds over grasslands. Moreover, ponies and donkeys in the pet category, especially those kept and fed in stables, are inevitably given more heat-producing foods than those fed on pasture. As a consequence the body becomes more heated and this accelerates the activity of the sweat glands.

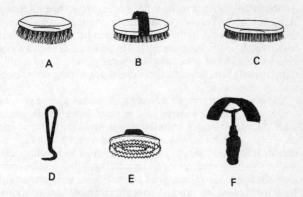

12. Grooming kit: (A) dandy brush; (B) body brush; (C) water brush;
(D) hoof pick; (E) rubber curry-comb; (F) sweat-scraper.

The purpose of regular grooming is not only to keep the coat clean but also to keep the skin clean, and to stimulate the sweat and oil glands. Brushing the coat to remove scurf also prevents the spread of skin diseases, which are encouraged by dirt on the coat and in the hairs.

Grooming can be done properly only with the correct equipment, which means an initial investment of several pounds. You can get quite cheap brushes and other items, but this is a false economy. Cheap brushes, for example, soon lose their bristles and have to be replaced. Good-quality brushes and other grooming equipment will give years of service if thoroughly cleaned after use and kept in a stout tin box. Do remember that everything stored in the grooming box must be absolutely dry before you put it away.

The minimum essentials for a grooming kit are: hoof pick, dandy brush, body brush, curry comb, water brush, sponge, stable rubber, sweat scraper, and mane and tail comb – some of these are illustrated in figure 12. The cheapest item of all is the wisp, which you can make yourself from straw. It is also a good idea to keep in the grooming box some plain lint and a roll of cotton wool. You will find these useful for wiping out the nose and eyes.

If it is your first pony or donkey and you have never groomed one before, you will have to gain its confidence before you can start. This can be done by talking to it, stroking it and offering an occasional titbit such as a lump of sugar or a piece of apple or carrot. It is a good idea to get in touch with a local riding stable and pay to have some lessons in grooming. When you feel confident that you can groom your animal, have someone hold its head for the first few times. Above all, you must have confidence and if you do feel nervous do not let the animal sense the fact. A pony or a donkey soon becomes nervous and restless in response to your nervousness. Be firm with the animal and it will soon learn that you are master or mistress of the occasion and will learn to do what it is told.

When you feel confident that you can handle the situation, lead the pony or donkey from its stable and, if no one is going to hold its head, tether it to a post or convenient tree. A proper tethering post is worth buying. There are some attractive wooden or metal ones with a horse's head on top. The post should be set firmly in the ground or in the concrete forecourt of the stable, if there is one.

The first stage in grooming is to examine the hooves carefully and use the hoof pick to remove dirt or stones from the cleft or between the hoof and the shoe. Work from heel to toe with the hoof pick and be careful not to press too hard. If there is something difficult to remove or the hoof seems unduly sensitive so that the animal jerks when you are probing, the cause of the discomfort could be serious and may require veterinary attention. *Never wash hoofs if they are dirty*; loose dirt is best removed with a stiff brush – a scrubbing brush will do very well.

A pony must be properly shod, so be sure to examine the hooves for any indication of a loose shoe, or for nails that have penetrated through the front of the hoof. The sides of the shoe should rest against the outside wall of the hoof. If the shoe is not resting properly, i.e. fitting and pressing on the sole of the hoof, the animal needs to have the shoe renewed. A misplaced shoe causes pressure on the sole of the hoof and can cause a painful corn. If a pony or donkey is frequently ridden on roads or other hard surfaces, it should be reshod every month. Sometimes the shoe is still serviceable but has become misplaced. In this event get the farrier to refit the shoe and at the same time trim the hoof. When a blacksmith tells you that new shoes are needed, accept his advice. A reputable blacksmith has a local reputation to maintain and he will not recommend reshoeing unless it is essential.

When you are satisfied that the animal's feet and shoes are in order, you can start grooming the body. You should begin at the head and work down to the tail. Should there be any lather or other indications of sweating, you will have to use the sweat scraper. The scraper is a long, flexible strip of metal in the form of a bow with a handle. Holding the scraper firmly, move it with sweeping motions along the sides of the neck, then along the flanks of the body, and finally down the rump. Continue doing this until all signs of sweat have disappeared.

Next, get to work with the dandy brush. This has bristles of stiff fibre. It is used to remove from the coat and legs any hard caked mud or other dirt. Should the dirt above the hooves be exceptionally hard, it can be softened with a little water and then brushed out.

Your next task is done with the body brush and the curry comb, which are always used together. The body brush has short stout bristles. On the back of the brush is a loop of webbing to keep it firmly on your hand and to prevent it from slipping. The purpose of the body brush is to remove scurf and dirt from the animal's coat. The curry comb is for clearing from the brush any bristles, hair and dirt collected while brushing. You will find that the body brush needs clearing about every sixth sweep across the coat.

There are two types of curry comb: the cavalry pattern and the jockey pattern. On both, the brush itself consists of a metal or, sometimes, a wooden base on which are mounted rows of blunt metal or rubber teeth. A jockey curry comb is fitted with a flat handle rather like that of a table-tennis bat. The cavalry curry comb does not have a handle, but has instead a web loop so that it can be secured to the back of the hand. This is much more convenient than the jockey type as it permits the palm of the hand to be placed on the animal's flank while using the body brush with the other hand.

The body brush is used with firm, circular sweeping motions for a few strokes all over the coat, constantly cleaning the brush on the curry comb. You will frequently have to clear the bristles of the curry comb by striking it sharply on the ground. Should there still remain on the coat some hardened dirt which was not removed by the dandy brush, it can be loosened by wetting and then a gentle application of the curry comb.

After finishing with the dandy brush and curry comb, there will remain on the coat dust raised by the brushing. This is removed with the water brush, which has longer and softer bristles than the dandy brush. Dampen the water brush and then apply it to the coat with long sweeps in the direction of the 'pile' of the hair. The water brush is also used for grooming the face and head, both of which are too sensitive for the dandy brush or the body brush.

When using any kind of brush to groom a pony or donkey be very gentle when applying them to the animal's stomach. The stomach is an extremely ticklish part of the animal anatomy and, if brushed too vigorously, the animal will start to kick! Also it will come to dislike grooming, which otherwise it would enjoy.

Having completed your brushing operations, clean the nostrils, lips and dock with the sponge, which should be dampened. Use damp cottonwool to clean the eyes and to remove any matter which may have collected in the corners. Tepid water should be used for eye-washing, and any strands of cotton wool left behind must be carefully removed. Examine the interior of the ears to see that they are clean. If they are not, wash them gently with damp cottonwool. Should you find any pimples or sores in the interior of the ears, it is wisest to get a veterinary surgeon to have a look at them. Satisfied that the interior of the ears are clean, use the water brush to brush out the inside and outside hairs of the ears, holding the tip of the ear between your forefinger and thumb.

The mane should be groomed by brushing the roots with the body brush to remove any scurf. Then comb out any tangled hair with the mane comb. This comb is of metal and has broad teeth. Finish off the mane with the mane brush. If the tail happens to be very dirty, it can be washed in a bucket of warm water containing soap flakes. When grooming the mane and tail avoid tugging them with the comb as you may break the hairs or pull them out. Finally smooth down the coat with the stable rubber, which can be a chamois leather or a piece of silk. This gives the coat an attractive shine.

If you have sufficient energy left, you can precede the use of the stable-rubber with a rub down with the wisp. The wisp is made by twisting lengths of hay into a rope about 8 feet long. A loop is made at each end of the rope. The wisp is pulled along the coat in the direction of the hair, but avoid using it on the head or loins. Wisping is not really essential every time you groom, but its occasional use does improve the appearance of the coat.

One word of warning: ponies and donkeys are rather sensitive on the inside of the thighs, so, when grooming these parts, grasp the hamstring with your free hand. This will guard against the animal suddenly kicking out.

Opinions differ about the advisability of giving a pony or donkey a bath. It must be done with fairly warm soap and water, and it takes a lot of time. The animal must then be hosed down to remove any soap clinging to the hair. After the animal is dry, it should be groomed in the ordinary way. Personally, I am against bathing a pony or a donkey, chiefly because of the difficulty of getting the coat thoroughly dry and the risk of the animal catching a chill. If dry grooming is properly done, there should be no need for a bath.

When you come back from riding, always remove any sweat and give the coat a quick rub-down. Then put a horse-blanket over the animal to prevent it from catching a chill. You can then stable it, and give it something to eat and a small drink of water.

There is little point in giving a pony a thorough grooming and then putting it back into a dirty stable. Cleaning a stable is the least pleasant of the chores necessary to the animal's well-being and comfort. Mucking-out is the term which adequately

describes stable cleaning. To do the job properly, you will need a four-pronged fork, a stable brush with a long handle, a wheel barrow and a length of hose with a nozzle. The bed provided for the pony or donkey should consist of straw or peat moss laid quite thickly and piled up round the edges. A bed laid in this way ensures that the animal is protected from draughts when it lies down and does not injure itself when it moves about.

Start cleaning operations by removing the bed. As it will be damp from urine and mixed with dung, use your fork to load it into the wheelbarrow to be tipped outside, well away from the stable. Used bedding makes good manure, which can be used for the garden or given to a local farmer. Some people are content just to fork the dung out of the bedding, which is then turned over with the fork and left lying for further use. Although this may save time in mucking out, I certainly cannot approve of it. Not only will some of the straw still be damp from urine and so spoil the coat when the animal lies down but also the stable will become smelly.

After the old bedding has been removed, thoroughly brush out the stable with the broom. Then connect the hose to the standpipe outside the stable and flush the floor with water. Give the floor a final brushing and let it dry out. The gulley in the floor leading to the drain will prevent the water used for flushing the floor from collecting outside the stable door and flooding the entrance. When brushing the floor after it has been flushed, be sure to brush from the walls towards the gulley and not from the back of the stable towards the door. When the stable floor is thoroughly dry, put down fresh bedding, tossing the straw about with the fork so that it falls in all directions. A clean stable is now ready to receive a freshly-groomed pony or donkey.

Chapter Seven

SOME HINTS ON RIDING

Before you think of buying a pony you must be able to ride one. Having a pony you cannot ride is like buying books when you cannot read. Just as the books will lie unopened on their shelves, so the pony will be useless to you in its field or stable. Therefore, learn to ride properly before you buy your own mount; then you and your pony will be able to establish the right kind of relationship and understand what is expected of each other.

There is also the matter of safety. If you buy a pony without knowing how to ride, you may be tempted to get on its back and dash off with disastrous results to yourself and other people. This type of behaviour is just as foolish as someone who cannot drive getting into a car and then careering down a main road. Learning to ride is not something you can teach yourself, neither will all the textbooks in the world teach you the art of riding. The only way to become a rider is on the back of a pony and doing what a qualified instructor tells you to do.

The purpose of this chapter is not to teach you riding, but to give you a few hints that may prove helpful when you go for your first riding lessons. But do not let your reading of the hints delude you into thinking that you are now a rider and confidently let your instructor think that you know all about riding. He will soon realize how little you really know about the practical side of riding once he has put you on the back of a pony.

One of the most difficult and, to the beginner, frightening things about learning to ride is getting on the animal's back. Yet there should be nothing difficult or frightening about mounting if you obey your instructor and go the right way about it. I will

68

assume that the pony has been saddled and bridled ready for
you. To mount, stand with your back to the head of the pony
and close to his shoulder. Now gather the reins up in your left
hand so that there is not a lot of slack between the bit and your
hand. Your next move will be to put your foot in the stirrup.

13. First stage in mounting a pony.

Turn the stirrup iron towards you with your right hand so that,
when you have mounted, the smooth flat edge of the stirrup will
rest against your leg. Then place your left foot in the stirrup so
that the bottom part or platform of the iron is against the heel of
your boot or shoe. You now have to hop on the ground with

your right leg until your body is at right angles to the pony (figure 13).

When you have got your body in the right position relative to the pony, press the toe of your left foot firmly down into the

14. Second stage in mounting.

stirrup iron until it is under the pony's chest and in line with the girth. Using your left hand, hold on to the tree or top front of the saddle. With your right hand grasp the back of the saddle, and with a quick spring swing your right leg over the saddle and place your right foot in the stirrup iron you will find there (figure 14).

Your instructor will probably insist on your practicing mounting a few times before you actually start riding. Also, the pony will be held by the head and you will be given a lift on to its back and into the saddle. But with practice you soon will gain confidence and be able to mount with complete assurance. After a few lessons you will wonder why you ever thought mounting was difficult.

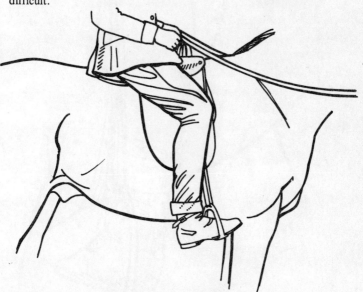

15. Correct position of foot in stirrup.

Once you are safely seated in the saddle, adjust you feet so that only the ball of the foot is in each stirrup. Then move the iron slightly to twist the stirrup leathers and so that the insides of the stirrups rest across the balls of the feet and against the arches of your feet on the inside (figure 16). This will prevent you from

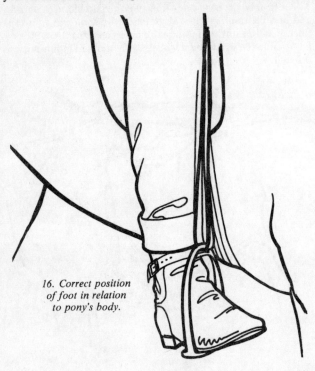

16. *Correct position of foot in relation to pony's body.*

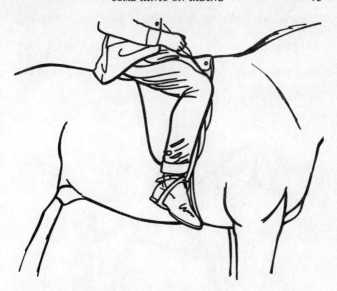

17. Incorrect position of foot in stirrup.

losing a stirrup through it coming off your foot if the pony makes a sudden, unexpected movement. The incorrect way to keep feet in stirrups is shown in figure 17.

Having got into the saddle with your feet correctly placed in the stirrups, you have to learn the right way to hold the reins. You will very likely be told to hold the reins in both hands at first, but with experience you will soon be able to hold them with one hand (figure 18). Satisfied that you are holding the reins correctly, your instructor will tell you to pull them very gently so that the pony feels them on the bit. Then say to the pony in a quiet but firm voice, 'Walk on', and as your mount begins to move press your heels against his ribs.

Good instructors are always very particular about a pupil sitting correctly on his or her mount. A good seat, as sitting in a saddle is called, makes all the difference between good and bad

18. How to hold a pony's reins correctly.

riding. A good seat means sitting well back in the saddle and with heels pressed well down. Not only is this the mark of a good rider, but it means that your legs will be comfortable and will stay that way throughout a long ride.

While you are riding the reins should be held about 10 inches above the front of the saddle and some 6 inches from your chest.

This sounds a bit complicated, but as your instructor will tell you, it is the most comfortable and least tiring position and at the same time gives you complete control of the horse through the bit. The reins should be held with your forefinger separating

19. Good riding seat

them, while your thumb presses on both reins. Your fist should be kept closed.

The speed at which you will ride your pony and the direction in which you want it to go are not, as is so often thought, solely controlled by using pressure or by pulling on the reins to convey your intentions through the bit. Your voice, the pressure of your legs on the animal's flanks, and changing the position of your body to shift its weight on the animals back are all as important, if not more important, than any use of the reins and bit. Incidentally, a good rider on a properly trained and responsive pony should have little need to apply spurs or a riding crop. A slight tap on the flanks with a whip or crop is sufficient to check any misbehaviour on the part of your mount.

Like all animals which for thousands of years have been closely associated with man, ponies and donkeys appreciate the sound of the human voice and are very sensitive to changes in its inflection. A pony likes to be talked to, but not shouted at, while it is being ridden. An animal that has been frightened or excited by some sudden sight or sound will often be calmed down if spoken to in a firm and reassuring tone of voice. In such circumstances, your voice can be more effective than pulling on the reins.

Using your legs properly is an important factor in guiding and controlling the movements of a pony. For example, pressure from your right leg will cause the pony to move his hindquarters to the left, while pressure from your left leg will have the opposite effect. The animals direction can be corrected by applying pressure from your leg against the flank opposite to that towards which the pony is straying.

Changing your position to shift your weight and therefore your centre of balance in the saddle causes a change in your mount's centre of balance. Leaning forward or backward in the saddle increases or decreases your weight on the hindquarters. A good riding instructor will explain exactly how changes of position in the saddle help to control your mount's movements and actions.

The various speeds at which a pony can be ridden all have appropriate names such as trot, walk, canter and gallop. It would be quite unsatisfactory to try and tell you in a book how to start or terminate these movements or how to change from one movement to another. You can learn these things properly only on the back of a pony with an instructor riding beside you to give directions and advice.

20. Cavalry method of dismounting—it is not recommended for beginners.

At the end of your riding lesson there comes the moment when you have to dismount. There is quite a simple method of doing this in absolute safety. Prepare to dismount by placing your outstretched arms along the sides of the pony's neck. Then stretch out your legs so that they are clear of the saddle and swing yourself on to the ground. Needless to say, you must remember to take your feet out of the stirrups before making the dismounting actions!

Another fairly simple method of dismounting is to take both feet out of the stirrups, then swing one leg over the front of the saddle. You then slide off the saddle to the ground. This takes some practice and must be done quickly and carefully without alarming the pony, otherwise it may move and you will end up in a heap on the ground. There is nothing more undignified than tumbling off a pony as you dismount.

21. Correct position at start of a jump.

If you have seen cavalrymen dismount, you will have noticed that the soldier leaves his right foot in the stirrup and swings his left leg over the saddle so that his left foot is on the ground. Until

22. Correct position at the end of a jump.

then he does not take his right foot out of the stirrup. This is undoubtedly the most graceful way to dismount, but it is not for the amateur: if something frightens the animal and causes it to move forward, you may not be able to get your left foot out of the stirrup before you are thrown off balance and dragged along the ground. It can, of course be done with either foot (figure 20).

No doubt, after you have learned to sit and to ride your pony correctly, you will be ambitious to try some jumps. Never

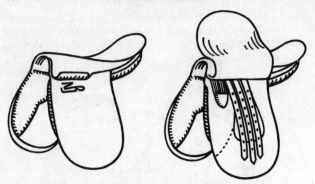

23. *Typical riding saddle for a pony; (right) with flap raised.*

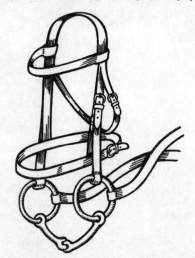

24. *Head harness showing bit attached to reins.*

attempt to do anything like this until your instructor is satisfied that you can handle a pony properly with its feet on level ground. The secret of good jumping lies in the pressure exerted on the bit by the reins and by the seat of the rider. Lean forward a little and slightly tighten the reins as you begin the jump (figure 21). As you come over the obstacle, slacken the reins and sit well

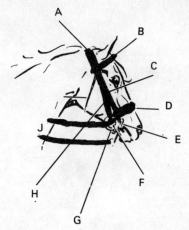

25. *Head harness on pony: (A) head stall; (B) brow band; (C) check piece (curb); (D) nose band; (E) curb; (F) curb chain; (G) snaffle; (H) cheek piece; (J) reins.*

back (figure 22). If you sit too far forward, you are liable to be tossed over your mount's head when its forefeet touch the ground. However, the technique of safe and expert jumping cannot be learned from books and requires constant practice and instruction.

Your pony will have to be provided with a saddle, a bridle and other equipment, but the price and variety of saddlery cannot be dealt with here. It is largely a matter of advice and individual preference. It is best to get advice from an experienced rider on both equipment and how to saddle and harness a pony.

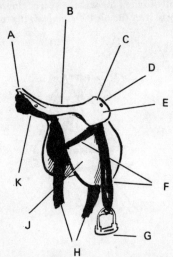

26. *Saddle placed on pony's back: (A) cantle; (B) seat; (C) pommel; (D) crutch; (E) skirt; (F) stirrup leather; (G) stirrup iron; (H) saddle girth; (J) flap; (K) panel.*

Riding clothes are another matter of individual preference, but for a youngster just beginning to ride I would suggest buying a pair of jodhpurs, which are based on the design of the trousers worn by the native horsemen of India and Pakistan. The advantage of jodhpurs for the young rider is that they can be worn with ordinary shoes. As the rider gets older and bigger, it is cheaper to replace a pair of jodhpurs than it is to rekit with breeches and riding boots.

Leather gloves should be avoided, because in wet weather the reins tend to slip through them. The most suitable gloves are the string variety, as they give the hands a firm grip on the reins whatever the weather. Riding gloves should be a size larger than those normally worn.

There is a wide choice of riding jackets. These have one or two vents at the back and pockets cut on the slant. Black, dark grey or a quiet tweed are most favoured.

By far the most important item in your riding kit is the cap. Remember that, if you are tossed and fall on your head, a soft hat will not proect you, so wear a proper riding hat of the jockey type. The cap, in black velvet, should have a safety chin-strap and a collapsible peak.

Chapter Eight

THE DONKEY

Most of the advice so far given in this book applies to the donkey just as much as it does to the pony. Both animals are so closely related that they interbreed freely, the resulting cross between a pony and a donkey being a mule. Until the end of the eighteenth century, the word 'donkey' was unknown and there were only wild asses and tame asses. Today the name of donkey is solely applied to the tame ass.

It is not difficult to distinguish a donkey from a pony. The donkey is in general smaller and some are smaller than a Shetland pony, but a well-bred and properly cared for donkey can be 16 hands, that is about five feet, high. Other marked distinctions between the pony and the donkey are the latter's long narrow ears, a mane that stands erect on the neck instead of falling over on one side as with the pony, narrow feet and a tuft on the end of the tail. The donkey's body colour is usually some shade of grey, and there are always black stripes down each shoulder and another along its back. Sometimes a donkey is brown or nearly black, while very occasionally a white specimen appears.

Wild asses, which are faster and more heavily built than the domestic donkey, roam in herds across the open plains of Africa and Asia. Being less demanding in their needs for food and drink than ponies, they manage to survive in what is virtually desert country. Wild asses vary in size from the tiny Onagars of Persia to the Kiangs of Tibet. The latter are very big animals and rather horse-like in build.

Primitive man domesticated the ass as a riding animal and as a carrier of his goods and chattels long before the horse ceased to be hunted as a source of food. It is probable that the ass began its long and patient life as a beast of burden in the mountain districts of Africa and Asia, where it could keep its footing far better than a pony could. Since time immemorial asses have been part of the Arab scene, and even in these days of cars, motor cycles and scooters these animals still carry vast loads on their strong backs just as they did in Biblical times. It was on an ass that Jesus Christ road into Jerusalem on the first Palm Sunday. Indeed, the ass has been honoured with the legend that the stripes on its legs and back form a cross to commemorate its part in that great moment in Christian history.

27. Onagar.

Besides using the ass as a beast of burden, people in some parts of the world eat its flesh, which is said to taste better than horse meat. The milk of the ass is also very nourishing, particularly for invalids. The hide can be tanned into exceptionally

28. Kiang.

strong leather and it is claimed to be the best material for drums. For centuries eastern musicians have made flutes from hollowed-out ass bones. Primitive man made the heads of battle-axes from ass shoulder-blades and, if you read your Bible, you will remember that Samson is said to have slain 1000 Philistines with the jawbone of an ass!

Although the donkey, as we now call the domesticated ass, is seldom employed in England, Scotland or Wales as a beast of burden, it still earns its keep in Ireland where it can be seen in rural districts carrying panniers of peat on its back. For monotonous work needing lots of patience, the donkey is generally more useful than the pony or horse. In the courtyard of Carisbrooke Castle in the Isle of Wight there is a very deep well from which the castle garrison used to draw their water by donkey-power. Today donkeys do this only as an attraction for tourists. Above the well is a big wheel with slats between two rims. The donkey walks along the slats and, in doing so, turns the wheel and raises the water. The donkeys have been trained to step out of the wheel immediately the bucket reaches the top of the well.

For some quite unjustified reason the name 'donkey' is a synonym for stupidity. Nothing could be farther from the truth. A properly trained pet donkey is just as intelligent and obedient as a dog, besides being remarkably responsive and affectionate to an owner who treats it properly. It is true that a donkey tends to be stubborn at times, but there is usually a good reason for any display of stubbornness, and it is up to the animal's owner to find out the cause and put matters right.

Most children enjoy their first ride on the back of a donkey at the seaside. They soon discover that strange affinity between donkeys and young children. So it is not long before the average child longs to have a donkey of its own. In many ways a donkey is a more suitable pet for a child than a pony and it is a safer animal for a youngster to ride. It is more sure-footed and is less-inclined to break into fast trots or to start cavorting as a badly-trained pony may do. Provided the child has been taught the rudiments of riding, a boy or girl of five will be perfectly safe on a donkey with some parental supervision. Indeed, I would always recommend a donkey as a youngster's first mount. Experience with a donkey will stand a boy or girl in good stead when he or she comes to riding a pony.

Apart from the opportunity it gives for riding, a donkey is a most attractive pet and it is more akin to a large dog about the place than is a pony. This is particularly true if the donkey is bought as a foal and allowed to grow up with a child. The most suitable donkey for a youngster is the so-called miniature. It

29. Donkey foal.

grows to a height of about 3 feet at the withers. A miniature donkey poses few problems regarding accommodation and its food requirements are similar to those of a pony, though in smaller quantities. It will live quite happily in a fairly large suburban garden provided certain precautions are taken to prevent it from wandering on to the roads or other people's property.

Some sort of shelter will have to be provided for the donkey in winter, but this does not need to be elaborate. A strong garden shed (figure 11, chapter 4) to give protection against rain and cold winds will be adequate. Provided a donkey is given plenty of love and is properly fed, it makes few demands on its owner and gives unlimited affection in return.

Should you decide to house your donkey in a proper stable, the types recommended in chapter 4 will be perfectly satisfactory, though it does not need to be on the same large scale as for a pony.

One thing *you must not do is to tether a donkey foal with a rope attached to a stake* driven into the ground. The youngster may tangle itself in the rope or trip over it and break a leg. If you want to confine the donkey, even temporarily, put it in its shed or stable or, better still, fence off a small corral in a corner of the garden. In fact, a small corral is a good idea for any donkey, if you do not want it to eat the garden flowers and shrubs. Of course, if you live in the country, you may be able to hire part of an adjacent field for the donkey. This also helps with the food problem, since donkeys are very fond of grass.

Remember, too, that donkeys are thirsty creatures. Make sure that there is always water available for the animal to drink when it wants to.

The donkey menu is much the same as that recommended in chapter 5 for ponies. The only exception is that crushed oats and the proprietory pony nuts must be given only occasionally as they tend to be too heating for donkeys. Otherwise, a donkey has a considerably more catholic taste than the average pony. Donkeys will gratefully accept as part of their diet thistles, garden prunings, lawn mowings, potato peelings and other vegetable scraps. As already advised for ponies, *never feed a donkey lawn mowings unless they are freshly cut.* If the mowings have been allowed to ferment at all, they will play havoc with the animal's digestion. Lawn mowings given to a donkey should be scattered on the ground so that it can browse on them. Cheese and dairy scraps make a welcome addition to the donkey menu, as does an occasional piece of cake. A lump of sugar can be given as a special treat or as a reward.

Never feed a donkey yew leaves as these are poisonous. Avoid also wheat and chicken feeds, though wheat products such as bran are quite safe. *Lupin and laburnum seeds are poisonous to donkeys, and on no account should they be given meat or any meat products.*

30. Broken-coloured donkey.

Unlike a pony, a donkey need not be shod, unless it is going to be walked or ridden on the road a great deal. If shoes are fitted, they must be removed every month or so and refitted to allow for growth of the hoof. While on the subject of hooves, do not attempt to trim them yourself when they appear to be overlong. Hoof-trimming is an expert and delicate operation, and should be performed only by a farrier.

Donkey foals must not be ridden, even by a child, however great the temptation. Putting weight on a young donkey will damage its back irretrievably. A young child can be allowed on a donkey's back when the animal is at least two years old. The young rider should not be permitted to stay on the donkey youngster for longer than a few minutes at a time. Should the mount show the slightest sign of discomfort, immediately remove the rider.

To keep a donkey's coat neat and in good condition does not require the prolonged and elaborate grooming given to a pony. Brushing once a day with a wire-bristled dog-brush is sufficient to keep the donkey coat smart and clean. Donkeys cast their coats in spring and it will help the appearance of the new coat if surplus hairs are removed by plucking. If a donkey gets its legs muddy, the dirt can be washed off, but be sure to dry the legs afterwards. Pay particular attention to drying the fleshy part of the heels. Leaving the heels damp after washing runs the risk of their becoming cracked or chapped.

One final piece of advice: make a donkey your companion in much the same way as you would a dog. Donkeys have a greater capacity for giving and receiving affection than ponies. A donkey left on its own all day without anyone speaking to it soon becomes miserable, and a miserable donkey is liable to develop vices which will make him unpopular. A donkey that has a relationship of love and understanding with its master or mistress is a happy and contented donkey that will give you many years of faithful companionship.

Chapter Nine

AILMENTS

No one without veterinary knowledge should attempt to treat a sick or injured pony or donkey. If your pony or donkey shows the slightest indication of being off-colour, lose no time in asking a veterinary surgeon to have a look at the invalid. There may be nothing seriously wrong with the animal, but it is better to pay the vet for a false alarm than to delay calling him and have a sick pony or donkey needing prolonged treatment instead of the single veterinary examination which would probably have cured the trouble.

Veterinary advice is particularly essential in the case of a seemingly sick donkey. A sick pony, like the average dog, will endure a great deal of pain and discomfort, and seldom loses its will to recover and live. However, a donkey sickening for something and which does not receive immediate expert attention is quite likely to wander off to find some place in which to die. So, *if your donkey appears to be in pain or sick, do not wait to see if it is better the next day*; call in the veterinary surgeon without delay. This does not mean that you should delay calling the vet to see a pony which appears to be ill or injured. The sooner the vet is called to the pony, the sooner it will be cured by expert treatment.

Veterinary advice being the first essential, therefore, this chapter is not intended to make you an animal home doctor. Its sole purpose is to indicate the alarm signals of something needing veterinary advice.

When a pony or a donkey seems unduly restless and takes little interest in what is going on around it, or even tends to ignore its master or mistress, you should suspect that something is wrong. Other indications that all is not well with an animal are: loss of weight; dull eyes; a tendency to mope around with the head held low; excessive sweating; loss of appetite; anything abnormal in the droppings, particularly looseness; dull and ragged coat; ill temper; or a ragged and staring coat. These are all signs that something is wrong.

The above are all initial warnings of something amiss and certainly merit calling in the veterinary surgeon. The following list of specific ailments and their appropriate symptoms help the vet to decide upon the invalid's treatment.

BUTTERCUP ALLERGY. In summer, when buttercups are in flower, grazing donkeys, particularly skewbalds, develop an allergy which causes the skin to peel around the nose and mouth. The neck glands swell and the invalid goes off its feed. Sometimes the sufferer becomes asthmatic. The trouble can be cured provided a veterinary surgeon is called in and the treatment he orders is followed rigidly.

COLIC. This is a severe attack of indigestion and, if you suspect it from the fact that the animal alternately lies down and gets up, and constantly turns to look at its stomach, lose no time in obtaining veterinary assistance. Colic can be symtomatic of something more serious.

CONSTIPATION. A sudden change in diet or incorrect feeding can cause constipation. It usually responds to a dose of linseed oil and a course of bran mashes including some fresh greens.

COUGHING. Another ailment on which veterinary advice is desirable. The cough may be temporary and harmless, but it could be the precursor of some serious disorder which only veterinary examination can diagnose and treat accordingly.

DIARRHOEA. This can be caused by sudden changes in diet or by an excess of sloppy foods. It normally clears up after a course of linseed jelly and a gruel, helped by a dose of castor oil. If the attack fails to respond to this treatment, consult a veterinary surgeon.

GLANDERS. This highly contagious diseases is indicated by small pimples on the animal's muzzle. The pimples later turn into ulcers. It is a case for calling the vet immediately and the disease must be reported to the police.

HERNIA. Indicated by a swelling in the groin. It can be put right by surgery. A neglected hernia can become strangulated and that can prove fatal.

INFLUENZA. A pony or donkey which suddenly goes off its feed and rapidly loses weight probably has contracted equine influenza. This needs immediate veterinary treatment. The disease is highly contagious to animals but not to humans. A case of influenza must be kept in strict quarantine.

LAMINITIS. The cause and symptoms of this complaint are described on page 40 in chapter 3.

LICE. Ponies and donkeys which have been grazing with other animals sometimes get lice. The lice tend to collect at the base of the hairs on the mane, tail and ears. Effective anti-louse dusting powders are on the market. The powders must be well rubbed into the roots of the hair. Care has to be taken to prevent the powder from coming into contact with the ears, eyes and nostrils. Equine lice cannot infest the human body.

LIVER DISORDERS. Yellowish tinge in the eyes, foul-smelling breath and a high temperature are symptomatic of liver trouble. Suspected liver disorders should be reported to the vet.

NAVICULAR. The causes and symptoms of this are described on page 41 in chapter 3.

NETTLERASH. Symptoms are a swelling on the body similar to that caused on humans by stinging-nettles. Nettlerash usually rights itself, but should it persist consult a veterinary surgeon in case the rash is symptomatic of something serious.

RINGWORM. Donkeys are not as susceptible to ringworm as ponies. The symptom is bald patches on the skin. The infected part is scurfy but is not surrounded by a red ring. If you suspect ringworm, lose no time in consulting a veterinary surgeon. There are various methods of treating the infection successfully.

SPLINTS. Symptoms and causes of this are described on page 41 in chapter 3.

SPRAINS. This subject is dealt with on page 41 in chapter 3.

STRANGLERS. This is highly contagious and requires immediate veterinary attention. The initial symptom is excessive swelling round the throat. In severe cases swellings will burst and discharge puss. Young animals are more susceptible, especially in the spring. The disease is rarely fatal if treated in time by a veterinary surgeon. Once an animal has had stranglers, it does not get it again.

SWEET ITCH. This is indicated by a rash developing on the crest, tail root and stomach. If the rash is untreated, the animal may scratch itself until it draws blood. Your veterinary surgeon will recommend a suitable lotion. Sweet itch is a form of eczema and normally occurs in summer on ponies and donkeys living in the open.

TEETH. As ponies and donkeys get older, the molar teeth frequently develop jagged edges that can injure the tongue. You should inspect the teeth regularly and, if you detect any rough edges, get your veterinary surgeon to file the offending molars. Jagged teeth are painful and hinder proper mastication of feeds, leading to digestive troubles.

TETANUS. Ponies and donkeys let out to pasture are liable to suffer scratches from posts and barbed wire. Although the injuries are in general trivial in themselves, they can lead to blood poisoning. Consequently, the animals should be given regular anti-tetanus injections by a veterinary surgeon.

WARTS. Although these can be unsightly, they are in general harmless, but it is essential that they are removed by a veterinary surgeon when they appear on any part of the body in contact with a saddle or other harness.

WHISTLING. The various ills of which this may be a symptom are dealt with on page 42 in chapter 3.

WORMS. Both ponies and donkeys are prone to worms. Consequently a thorough worming in spring and autumn is a wise precaution. Your veterinary surgeon will advise on the most suitable worming medicine to use and how it should be administered. No animal should be ridden immediately after worming.

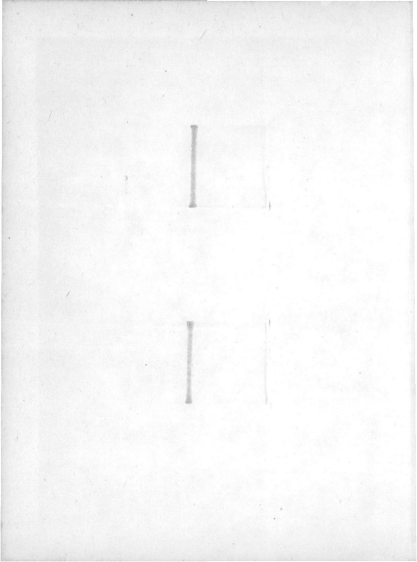